# Job Search Journal

*A Step-by-Step Guide For Job Hunters and
Career Changers
With Worksheets to Track Progress for
Accountability*

# Table of Contents

# Introduction

It has been reported in various business websites, news stations, newspapers and social media that the US unemployment rate is at around 13.3% as of May 2020. That means 86.7% of the working population is employed. The bad news is you might be, or might know someone, who is still a part of the remaining 13.3%. Unfortunately, things are even more uncertain nowadays with COVID-19. As workers, things are even more uncertain than ever.

Now, with the competition that includes knowledge, experience, personality and determination as the main criteria for judging, you have to prove yourself worthy of a position in that small group of lucky individuals who have a job. It does not matter if you have been laid off, you resigned or a fresh graduate; what is important is that you want the bosses to know what you are capable of.

If you have been looking around and trying for quite some time now but is still not getting that offer, you might want to revamp your plans.

This guide aims to help you find and get that job you have always dreamed of. It will guide you through the whole process of job-hunting: from the searching, to preparing your documents, the interview and whatever comes next. These are proven effective ways on how to get a job in 30 days without sacrificing your passion or talent.

In the end, I want to help you maximize your potential and your resources. Not being offered a job does not mean you are not good. It may just be that it is not the right job for you, or you are not selling yourself the right way. Either way, I am here to help you.

# Chapter 1: Get Yourself Prepped

After you have left a job or graduated college, the most sensible thing to do is to look for a job that will suit not just your financial needs, but your career growth needs as well.

Naturally, unless you would rather start your own line of business, you would want to look for a job that will pay enough to keep you ahead of your bills, offers insurance and 401(K) plan for your future, will continuously challenge you to make yourself better in your chosen field, and will recognize your potentials. We look for so many things in a job without asking ourselves, is the job looking for me? Sometimes, we tend to focus on what we want but neglect some facts that the job wants.

**Back to Basics**

Before going further, look into some of the words or phrases below and remind yourself of what they mean:

Job Advertisement – This refers to an advertisement about a job opening. You may see these ads posted on social media pages, classified ads, job boards or on TV or radio. As it is an advertisement after all, it aims to attract applicants with things such as "Competitive Salary Offer of up to $2,500.00/month" or "Are you Intelligent and Hardworking? Join the best Company in Town NOW." These ads may be or may not be true, but be very careful and read each single word in the job posting itself.

Job Description – This will give you the essentials about a specific job, including the job title, location, working conditions, duties, hazards, etc.

Duties and Responsibilities – This lists down all the functions and responsibilities of the person who will fill in the vacancy. For example:

- Reports directly to the General Manager

- Will be required to prepare financial reports and marketing plans

Job Requirement or Qualification – This refers to everything that the job will ask of you. It includes work experiences, a specific set of skills, professional certifications, educational credentials, etc. For example:

- A minimum of 5 years work experience in the same capacity is required.

- Must have above average English communication skills.

Now, look again at that job posting. Do you think it is asking for you? Understanding every information provided in a job advertisement will give you the information you need and help you decide if this is the job you are looking for. It is very important that before you apply for anything, you understand what is expected of you. This essential part is what the job seeker usually forgets about.

**Most Common Job-seeking Mistakes**

Many people probably think that mistakes can only be committed during the process. No. Even before one starts looking for a job, it is already possible to commit mistakes. Here are some of the most common mistakes job seekers often do, consciously or not.

1. Taking a long or too many vacations.

   So after quitting your job or being laid off, what do you do? Although it is normal to take a quick breather before getting yourself out there again, it is not going to do you any good if you take more than a month before looking for another job. Taking breaks after each process is also a red flag for employers. Taking very long breaks will actually put you into lazy mode. What usually happens is you enjoy too much and forget about your will to look for another job.

Now, having breaks in between each process says you are not very eager to take the job. For example, after your interview, it took you more than a week before submitting the needed supporting documents, or when the HR called you to schedule an interview, you requested it to be a month later.

2. Not having the time.

   Recent study shows that around 44% of job seekers around the world only dedicate around 2 to 3 hours of their time looking for a new job. Now, imagine if you dedicate more time to job-hunting since you do not have a present job anyway. After walking in to an office and submitting your resume, they said they would get back to you if you were shortlisted.

   You can use that time to go to a local employment agency and see what they have in their job board, update your LinkedIn profile, visit the Careers page of a company website or go to job portals online.

3. Focusing on just one vacancy.

There is nothing wrong with aiming for the best position available to you, but the problem is what if it does not work out as you wanted it to? Experts suggest that your job-seeking efforts should not stop after your preferred employer has invited you to an interview.

It is best to continue looking for opportunities and showing up on interviews until you hear from the employer of your choice. Should they not call you for that offer, at least you have other options.

4. Not reviewing your resume.

You made that, and you are pretty confident that everything is written perfectly to the best of your ability. Even so, it is best to ask for other people's second opinion. Ask a trusted friend or family, or someone with a background on recruiting or interviewing applicants then show them your resume. Let them look for typos, misspelled words, unimportant information or important skills that you have not provided. Also, be open to constructive criticisms.

Lastly, ask them, "Based on my resume, if I am to apply in your company as a _____, would you hire me?" Their honest, unbiased response will give you an idea of how effective your resume is.

5. Not tailor fitting your resume.

Your time and effort to make sure that your resume is tailor-fitted to the needs of the company you are applying at will definitely pay off when your employer does not have to figure out why they should hire you. If you have a wide range of experiences, make sure that the resume you are sending to a prospective employer has already been made according to what they are looking for.

The downside of sending generic resume or curriculum vitae is that the employer would have to look through your whole document and try to look for the things that fit his needs. This takes time, something that an employer does not have a lot of.

6. Spending all of your time looking for a job.

Yes, we said earlier that you have to dedicate a lot of your time to your job search, but that does not mean not having a social life. Remember that your family, friends, or the new people you meet can be the answer to your prayers. They may know someone or they may actually be looking for someone like you who can deliver the job they need.

A day or two to socialize will actually do you good, but still know your priorities, and be careful not to do anything crazy during those days, or you might just lose the chance being given to you.

7. Providing inaccurate information.

This could be the worst thing you can do during the process. Providing potential employers with not-so-true information can backfire in the worst way possible. You cannot either exaggerate your abilities or provide something that has never happened. Trust me; they have ways to know more about these inaccuracies. Make sure that you can live up to every information you provide.

If you say that you have worked and have been commended for so many times and at the time of the interview and background check, the employer finds out that this is rather the opposite, then expect your application to go straight to the shredder. Although there would be times when your potential employer can give you a chance to redeem yourself, it is better to just stick to what is true and realistic.

When you are trying to bounce back and look for better opportunities, you want to make sure that you are doing everything you can and you are maximizing the time you have to make it happen. Although the saying "good things come to those who wait" holds true in most aspects of one's life, it is just not going to happen like that in job-hunting.

You have to look for it. Remember that the competition is stiff and to get ahead, you have to make yourself visible and on the right path.

**What to Do?**

*Step 1: Relax*

Do this for the first couple of days in your 30-day job-hunting plan. Do everything that will set your senses at peace. Savor this moment and make sure that by the time you are done, you have fully regained your energy to find a job and be a part of the workforce again.

*Step 2: Self-assessment*

Before applying for a job, it is expected that you are of sound mind, body and spirit to perform the tasks required by the position you are applying for so it is best to ask yourself the following questions:

1. Are you ready to attend interviews?

2. Are you ready to start immediately if ever you get hired?

3. Are you ready for possible rejection and look for another opportunity?

4. Are you ready and willing to relocate and travel should the position require?

*Step 3: Prepare your Documents*
Now that you are ready to look for your next awesome job, you would need your documents. The next step is to get these things ready. All documents containing your employment history, education and identification such as certificate of employment or recommendation letters, government ID, social security card/number, working visa (if applicable) etc. should be placed in just one envelope. That way, you would not have to search the whole house again to look for them.

## Chapter 2: Planning and Targeting

Before anything else, ask yourself one question: are you ready now? When you leave a job, it is actually expected that you will spend a week or two to rest your mind and your body, and there is absolutely nothing wrong with that. If you have had problems with your previous employer or if you have resigned because of emotional and physical stress, this will help you get yourself ready for the next opportunity that fits your needs best.

It is not advisable to look for a job the next day after you left your job because that may cause you to be a bit emotional and the frustration may not work for your advantage.

Studies show that one of the biggest and most common mistakes of job seekers is that they grab the first opportunity that comes their way without thoroughly thinking about it. That means clicking the "Apply Now" button without reading the fine prints (the job description and qualification) or submitting a resume in an office that offers any job, as long as it is a job.

The end of this kind of process is dissatisfaction in the part of the employer as well as the employee.

**Assessing Yourself**

It is very important to know your own abilities. It is also the very first thing you want to do before finally going out there to find a new and better job. So what do you need to know about yourself? You can actually ask your colleagues, your friends or family's help for this step. All you need to do is to ask them

First, what skills do you have? List all the things you can and cannot do, your actual experiences, the trainings you have attended and of course, your college degree. The importance of knowing your capabilities cannot be stressed enough, but this will be your set-off point.

You have to be familiar with your skills and experiences so you can look for a job that will utilize and maximize your talents as well as continuously improve whatever you already have.

**Now that you already know what** you can do, ask yourself, what do you want to do? Does your set of skills and experiences go well with the job description you are looking at? Look for a job at an industry you are passionate about. The thing about choosing something you actually love is that your enthusiasm and passion about the job will emanate from you naturally, as compared to choosing something you do not really like but sounds good.

Now, set your goal. What kind of job are you looking for? Are you looking for a job that pays well, or a job that is going to give you more challenging responsibilities? Do you want a job near your home or are you willing to relocate? What is your expected salary? Is it going to be an essential path in your career goal?

As soon as you have all the answers to these questions and you already have a clear picture of what you are and how you will be, then it is time to start with the process. Refer to the last chapter of this guide for a job tracking journal to keep yourself accountable along the way. The act of writing things down and keeping track or your progress will motivate you in the long run.

NOTE: Never apply for a job that you are not really interested in or a position you are unlikely to be shortlisted for, just for the sake of finding a job. Aside from being a total waste of time, you are also likely to get out of the company soon if you do not really like and understand what you are doing.

**What is your Target?**

It is not a surprise if you already have a company in mind that you want to work for, but remember that you cannot focus on just one, no matter how confident you are that you are going to get the job. Since you have already established the job that you are looking for, you want to list down as much employers' name as possible, employers and companies that have job openings in the particular field you are interested in, or the specific job you are looking for.

It is best to do a quick research about the company you are targeting. Know their vision and mission statements. What are their philosophies? How do they uphold their social responsibilities? How do they take care of their people? What are their products and services? This will give you an idea of how your potential workplace would be like and what the company is like.

This can also provide you with enough information to help you decide if you really want to be a part of this company's team or not. Mind you, sometimes, the big companies do not share the same vision as you do and you might find everything you are looking for in smaller companies so just keep your eyes open for possibilities.

After targeting, you want to plan your course of actions. This includes the when, where, how and who. When will be the best time to talk to someone from this company to know more about their vacancy? Where will you find the correct information? How will you approach them to introduce yourself and what you have to offer and who should you look for?

**What to Do?**

Step 1: Assess your skills

After preparing yourself, you would want to re-assess your skills and experiences. What jobs will be a perfect fit for you? Do not waste your time sending applications for jobs that do not require your skills and experiences because there is a big possibility that you will not get an interview because you are not the person they are looking for.

Step 2: Do your research

The internet is full of information that just needs probing. Know what jobs will be perfect for you and your skills or which ones are in demand. When you finally made up your mind of which careers to pursue, you might want to look around for possible employers.

Get to know them by looking at their About Us page. Do a research about their products and services, their specialties, their working environment and their culture.

# Chapter 3: Knowing your Resources

How do you plan to look for a job? According to Forbes.com, another common mistake committed by job seekers is that they only focus on one job source. Most may just find it inconvenient to look elsewhere but you are likely to treasure a job more if you got the job from determination and hard work.

## Online Job Portals

One of the most convenient ways to look for a job is through online job portals or job boards, where different employers post job vacancies in just one website. One can compare this to a yellow pages found online specifically for jobs. Although this is your easiest ticket to your next job, it is going to be best for those applying for positions posted that have the exact qualifications the job ad is looking for.

The problem in most online job portals is that if the software or system used cannot find the keyword specified by the employer, it automatically disregards your application.

Examples of these job boards are Indeed.com, SimplyHired.com, Glassdoor.com, Monster.com and USAJobs.com.

## Classified Ads

Many employers still advertise vacancies in your daily newspaper. Although limited information are provided in these job ads, it will still give you more options that are sometimes not posted elsewhere.

## Company Websites

These are somehow like job boards but more exclusive to a specific company. If you have a specific employer in mind, then this will work fine for you. All you need to do is go to their website, go to their Careers page and look for their latest vacancies. Just remember to tailor your resume according to what they are looking for because just like in job boards, you may not be shortlisted if the software cannot find the keywords that it is looking for.

## Walk-in Applications

Sometimes, when you are out of places to go or you are already in a commercial space with lots of offices, walking in and submitting your resume personally always makes an impression. If you are lucky, you can have the initial interview on that same day.

## Social Media

Yes, even social media can help you find a job. If you are into Facebook, you can use that to your advantage. Recreate your page to make it look more professional. Choose you wall posts wisely and it might be best to keep some of your photos and videos private. You can also join groups of other job seekers as they may have tips or even leads for you. This will also give employers information about your interests and such.

**Your Personal Network**

It has already been mentioned that your family and friends, and their family and friends, can play a big part during your job-hunting days. Aside from the fact that they keep you sane during these tiring days, they may have information about job vacancies. If they do not have any lead yet, all you need to say is that you are looking and to let you know if they know anyone or see anything somewhere.

A person's ability to find a job is not the question here. Anyone can find a job anywhere. It is his willingness to go through the process, no matter how rocky the road is, and his carefully planned strategy that will take him there.

**What to Do?**

*Step 1: Update your LinkedIn*

If you do not have a LinkedIn (LinkedIn.com) account yet, it is time to create one. Research shows that LinkedIn.com is the most used social media site by employers when it comes to finding out more about an applicant. LinkedIn is a site where you can update your job experiences and educational background, build your professional connections, and get recommendations from friends and past and present colleagues.

*Step 2: Build your network*

Introduce yourself to possible leads. Ask your friends if they know anyone or saw an ad about job openings and ask for more details.

*Step 3: Make a list*

Take note of the job vacancies you found that interest and suit you. List down every information you can get about these positions and the company and stick to that list. This will guide you throughout the process so you will not go astray and apply for something that you are not cut out for.

*Step 4: Strategize*

Look at the job ads you found and plan your approach. That is, how will you market yourself? Some experts suggest cold calling your potential employer to set-up an appointment to introduce yourself and the services that you can offer to the company. Be very cautious about the company's preference, though. Although some prioritize walk-in applicants, some want their applicants profiled online. Have an approach tailor-fitted to the company's preferences.

*Step 5: Maximize your time*
List down all online applications that may be done in just one sitting. When you are walking in, be ready with a list of company addresses and schedule appointments for companies within the same area in a day. You may want to allot two to three hours per appointment to give a leeway for possible delays or just to help you get ready. If it is just not going to work for you with lots of appointments in one day, you may set it in different days; just make sure you will be able to attend them.

# Chapter 4: Building your Portfolio

Now that you have an idea of what you want to do and how to do it, it is high time to start building or updating your portfolio. Now, let us look on how you can make your job application documents even better.

**Cover Letter**

This is the first page of your document that the employers usually take a look at. This is usually sent to an employer together with a copy of a resume or curriculum vitae (CV), and it provides more information about the applicant. You can take it as an answer to possible interview questions, but in written form.

The cover letter includes basic information such as your complete name, how did you find out about the vacancy, your most relevant skills and experience, why are you interested in the job and why are you interested to work for the company.

There are five basic types of cover letters:

1. Value Proposition Letter - This explains the attributes that make a candidate unique and perfect for a position.

2. Referral Letter – A letter of application that includes the name of the person who gave you the information about the job opening.

3. Prospecting Letter – Sometimes called letter of interest, prospecting letter expresses interest about a specific job or inquires about the company's job vacancies.

4. Application Letter – This is the type of cover letter written for specific job applications.

5. Networking Letter – This seeks for job assistance or advice regarding applications and the likes from professionals or recruitment experts.

For the purpose of this guide's discussion points, let us focus our attention on application letters.

Your application letter should not only introduce you to the one reading it. It should also persuade the reader to proceed in reading your resume. It should be brief and straightforward, all written to fit just one page. In writing your cover letter, remember these things:

1. Customize. Do you remember how not tailoring your resume can negatively affect your application? Same goes with your cover letter. Each letter should be customized; each showcasing your knowledge about the responsibilities of the position and what set of skills is the company looking for.

2. Know your receiver. Who are you going to send it to? As much as possible, use the name of the person who will receive and take care of your letter. It is better to address the letter with "Dear Mr. Flint," instead of "Dear Ma'am/Sir" or "To whom it may concern." In case you have no way to find out who the addressee is, take the time to call the company to ask them to whom should you send your application to. It shows your genuine interest about the job.

3. Do more research about the job. If you can get enough information about the job in the ad, then good for you. Otherwise, you can actually talk to the person you are addressing your letter to and ask him/her everything you need to know about the job.

4. Research about the company, too. There may be times when you really like the job but do not know enough about the employer/s or maybe you already have a particular company in mind. Either way, it is best to find out more about the company's profile, what they stand for and what it is like to work for them.

5. Proofread. Whatever written document you will be sending, make sure that it has already been proofread and crosschecked

for possible typos, grammar lapses and other possible errors.

One reminder when writing your resume: never mention your pending job application to other companies. No matter how honest it is or how "in-demand" you may sound, remember that you are trying to convince them that you are serious about you application and that their company is your priority. Also, try to steer away from just repeating everything from your resume. Think of your cover letter as a summary of everything in your resume plus the reasons that make you a perfect candidate for the position.

Lastly, do not forget to include your contact information. Basically, you might want to include your primary phone number, e-mail address, mailing address, or any other means that they can contact you. Also, ask them to let you know should they need more information about you and those that you have done in the past.

## Your Resume

Think of your resume as your personal brochure. It helps you market yourself and present you in a positive light. Unfortunately, no matter how good you are or how incredible your accomplishments were, you still have to make sure your resume is well written.

You probably know this already but as a friendly reminder, a resume should include your contact information, an opening statement (usually an executive summary that tells the employer what you are looking for and who you are) and a list of all essential skills required by each specific job application. It should also include your educational background, your employment history and your character references.

So what should you avoid when writing your resume?

1. Inconsistent branding. If you are using your full name, make sure that it is going to be the same for all the documents you will be submitting, as well as the web pages that contain your professional profile.

2. Providing contact information that is not your own. If you are qualified for a position, they will keep in touch. When that happens, you want to be the first one to receive the information and they also expect to hear from YOU. It is not going to be good for you if you will indicate a phone number or email address that you have no control over.

Also, if you do not have it yet, try creating a more professional email address, for example, using your name or initials. If your email address is inappropriate, for example toohot4u@gmail.com or lilcutiepie@aol.com, employers might not take you seriously.

3. Including a generic career objective. Chances are, the employer already knows that you are "a professional who is looking for an opportunity that will help me apply and improve my skills." Firstly, they would not want someone who will only take their company as a training ground. Secondly, it is a waste of space. Instead, include an executive summary, a three to five-sentence paragraph explaining your capabilities, your core competencies and how you can be an asset to the company.

4. Events arranged in random order. The best way to present your employment and education history is to start from the most recent down to the earliest. If you have a lot to enumerate, stick to the ones that happened within the past 10 years. Remember that your employer does not have all day to read a 10-page resume so try to limit yours to two or three pages. If the experience is not relevant to the job you are applying for, take it off.

5. Not using professional language. Unlike giving presentations where you have to stick to simpler words that are easy to understand, using professional language in your resume is going to help you. This shows that you speak the same language as they are and if the terms are used in job postings, you will have more chances to pass the initial screening.

6. Using fancy formatting. Never use fancy and hard-to-read fonts in your documents. Aside from the fact that it is distracting and somehow unprofessional, it can also tire the reader's eyes. Stick to simpler fonts like Tahoma or Calibri. Also, avoid providing information in a block of texts. Present your achievements in bullet form and while you are at it, make sure to present them in a result-cause manner.

7. Including photos, tables and other images, as well as headers and footers. They are unnecessary.

8. Using pronouns in descriptions of accomplishments or job responsibilities. It is already a given that you wrote your own resume. So why still use "I" or "she" or "the applicant?"

9. Not providing quantified achievements. Instead of just saying, "generated highest

recorded sales income for the year 2013," why not include the actual amount? Although you will not need more than three bullets for this, an achievement with an actual figure is more believable and confident.

## Supporting Documents

This may include, but is not limited to, any of the following:

- Clearance or proof of employment from your previous employer

- Transcript

- Training certificates

- Licenses

- Recommendation letter

- List of references

- Social security card, national ID or any proof of identification

Before going out to send your resumes, be sure to have every document ready, with back up copy printed out or saved in your flash drive or cloud device. This will really help you speed up the process when the employer asks for them, instead of having to come back some other day or time to submit it. This will also show them how ready and eager you are to get that offer.

**What to Do?**

*Step 1: Update your resume and cover letter*
Make sure your resume is up to date and well written. Counter check it just to make sure that there are no grammar lapses, typos and misspelled words. Add your most recent job and achievements in your resume. Do not forget to customize. If possible, have different folders or envelopes for each company you are applying at to make sure that everything they need, including your customized resume, is in just one place to avoid confusion. Make sure they are for the right company and label each folder with the company's name and address.

*Step 2: Print and photocopy*
You will need several copies of your documents as required by the employer. Have them ready by printing them out or having them photocopied. If needed, call the company's HR to know which documents they need and have these ready days before your actual appointment.

## Chapter 5: The Interview

Some people consider this as the final step, while others will consider this the most terrifying part of the process. Either way, like what we have done with the previous steps, you just need a little practice and more information on how you can excel in your job interview.

If you have reached the interview portion of your application, you should congratulate yourself because you have already passed the initial screening and you are in the employer's "top list." While some pass interviews without so much effort, others still struggle with this final step.

Here is what you need to do to help you during the interview:

1. Practice. Of course, you do not know the exact questions the interviewer might ask you so what you can do is to rely on what's available in the internet. Look for common questions in job interviews. Ask a friend, colleague or relative to do the practice with you. Make sure that the person has experience in interviewing or recruitment so he/she can provide you with tips that you can use and provide you some points for improvements and solutions to address them.

2. Improve your communication skills. We do not need to be in an interview to do

this, but doing it for the interview's sake can actually help. Employers look for people who can communicate effectively; not just talk in front of people but to use all possible media to get a point across, no matter who the audience is. It is best to minimize the use of filler statements like "you know" or "well" if they are not necessary. Be mindful of your body language too, as they can send the wrong signals.

3. Dress-to-kill. Treat each interview as the first and last time you will see the interviewer. That way, you would have the drive to make and leave a good impression. This will include your choice of clothes, the color you choose to wear, the loudness of your make-up, the perfume you wear, etc. Remember that the first impression is made the moment you come into a room; the second is when you open your mouth. Wearing make-up is advisable, as you do not want your interviewer to think that you did not put enough effort to look presentable.

4. If you know that you usually fidget on interviews, try to calm yourself down before your call time. Come to the interview venue an hour or 30 minutes before your schedule so you can take some time to calm yourself and get

yourself familiar with the place. This can really help with the nerves.

5. Be aware of trick questions. If the interviewer asks you for something negative, for example, what are your weaknesses, you can be honest. Of course, your weakness is negative, but you can turn it around by enumerating ways that you have been doing to address the issue. You can also say that this weakness is not very negative after all; for example, saying that your weakness is that sometimes you get too hyped up and focused on a task and you forget some things that you wanted to do for yourself. Never let a question that requires a negative answer pass you by without turning it around and making it still sound positive in some way.

6. Do not let the interviewer's mood get the best of you. Sometimes, when we are too nervous and when we face someone intimidating, we tend to lose our grip. If you think the interviewer seemed to be having a bad day, try to flash a genuine smile and introduce yourself followed by "how are you doing today?" Try your best to lighten the mood; it is going to be good for the both of you.

7. After the interview, do not forget to thank the interviewer for meeting with

you and sparing you some of his/her time. Encourage your interviewer to contact you if he/she needs more information and to keep you updated if possible. Sending a Thank You email or voice message is also a good idea.

8. Keep in touch. Show your employer that you are really serious about your application by keeping in touch with them and asking for some updates about the results of your interview, and the next step that you need to go through.

## What to Do?
*Step 1: Practice*
Think of your interview as the ultimate performance of your life. Practice your introduction as well as your answers to possible questions. Record your voice and assess how you sound, aiming for 'confident, positive and pleasant.' Make sure that you sound lively and avoid memorizing your answers because interviewers have means of knowing if your answers are pre-medicated.

Practice with a friend and let him take note of your body language and your answers, and find ways to correct actions that may create a negative impact.
*Step 2: Have everything ready*

Prepare everything from the bag you will bring, the documents you will need, the clothes you will wear and your lucky pen. You do not want to forget anything so have them ready and accessible so you can just grab them and go.

*Step 3: Set your alarm*

Career coaches recommend that when going in an interview, it is best to be an hour early because it will give you time to relax before the interview. Leave home early as well to give allowance to possible delays.

*Step 4: Take notes*

After each interview, write down the questions you were asked and your responses. It is going to be really helpful for your future interviews.

*Step 5: This is your time to shine*

There are two types of interview questions: a. technical questions, and b. psychological or personality (HR) questions. Whatever types of question thrown at you, your answers should show your ability to think quickly, willingness to learn things and your expertise.

## Chapter 6: The Wait

Now that you are finally done, you are stuck to the phase where all you can do is wait. While waiting, you can still send applications to other companies. The most agonizing part of your waiting is that you do not know how you did during the process. Unfortunately, some recruiters will just tell you, "we'll call you in two weeks" or "we'll keep you posted" but not receive anything. Although this does not really mean you failed, it is just wise to prepare yourself.

1. Do not stop looking for other opportunities. Your search only stops when you stop looking. With the number of companies springing out everywhere, it is almost impossible not to find anything. However, you have to be patient and keep your momentum going. Research shows that people who do not stop looking or jobs actually get hired sooner so just keep looking.

2. Do not let failure dampen your spirits. It is okay to be sad if you do not get accepted in a company you have been dreaming of, but it's not okay to lock yourself because of depression and stop the search altogether. Stopping every time you fail will only prolong you job-searching agony.

3. If self-help did not work for you the first time, try getting professional help next time. Try going to an employment agency who can help you customize your portfolio according to what their clients are looking for. Just be informed of possible fees and payroll schemes that will apply to you should you go through them. Note that not all employment agencies are the same so if you do not agree with the terms of the first one or if their vacancies do not interest you, try another agency.

4. Try to assess your own performance and give yourself an unbiased feedback. Look for areas of improvement and try to work on that for the next interviews or resume writing to come.

# Chapter 7: Job Search Journal

# Job Application Tracker

Company :
Position :
Location:
Channel :
Notes:

**Y N**
**Interview :**
**Follow-up :**

---

Company :
Position :
Location:
Channel :
Notes:

**Y N**
**Interview :**
**Follow-up :**

---

Company :
Position :
Location:
Channel :
Notes:

**Y N**
**Interview :**
**Follow-up :**

---

Company :
Position :
Location:
Channel :
Notes:

**Y N**
**Interview :**
**Follow-up :**

# Job Application Tracker

Company :
Position :
Location:
Channel :
Notes:

**Y N**
**Interview :**
**Follow-up :**

Company :
Position :
Location:
Channel :
Notes:

**Y N**
**Interview :**
**Follow-up :**

Company :
Position :
Location:
Channel :
Notes:

**Y N**
**Interview :**
**Follow-up :**

Company :
Position :
Location:
Channel :
Notes:

**Y N**
**Interview :**
**Follow-up :**

# Job Application Tracker

Company :
Position :
Location:
Channel :
Notes:

**Y N**
**Interview :**
**Follow-up :**

---

Company :
Position :
Location:
Channel :
Notes:

**Y N**
**Interview :**
**Follow-up :**

---

Company :
Position :
Location:
Channel :
Notes:

**Y N**
**Interview :**
**Follow-up :**

---

Company :
Position :
Location:
Channel :
Notes:

**Y N**
**Interview :**
**Follow-up :**

#  Job Application Tracker

Company :
Position :
Location:
Channel :
Notes:

**Y N**
**Interview :**
**Follow-up :**

Company :
Position :
Location:
Channel :
Notes:

**Y N**
**Interview :**
**Follow-up :**

Company :
Position :
Location:
Channel :
Notes:

**Y N**
**Interview :**
**Follow-up :**

Company :
Position :
Location:
Channel :
Notes:

**Y N**
**Interview :**
**Follow-up :**

# Job Application Tracker

Company :
Position :
Location:
Channel :
Notes:

**Y N**
**Interview :**
**Follow-up :**

---

Company :
Position :
Location:
Channel :
Notes:

**Y N**
**Interview :**
**Follow-up :**

---

Company :
Position :
Location:
Channel :
Notes:

**Y N**
**Interview :**
**Follow-up :**

---

Company :
Position :
Location:
Channel :
Notes:

**Y N**
**Interview :**
**Follow-up :**

# Job Application Tracker

Company :
Position :
Location:
Channel :
Notes:

**Y N**
**Interview :**
**Follow-up :**

Company :
Position :
Location:
Channel :
Notes:

**Y N**
**Interview :**
**Follow-up :**

Company :
Position :
Location:
Channel :
Notes:

**Y N**
**Interview :**
**Follow-up :**

Company :
Position :
Location:
Channel :
Notes:

**Y N**
**Interview :**
**Follow-up :**

# Job Application Tracker

Company :
Position :
Location:
Channel :
Notes:

**Y N**
**Interview :**
**Follow-up :**

Company :
Position :
Location:
Channel :
Notes:

**Y N**
**Interview :**
**Follow-up :**

Company :
Position :
Location:
Channel :
Notes:

**Y N**
**Interview :**
**Follow-up :**

Company :
Position :
Location:
Channel :
Notes:

**Y N**
**Interview :**
**Follow-up :**

# Job Application Tracker

Company :
Position :
Location:
Channel :
Notes:

**Y N**
Interview :
Follow-up :

---

Company :
Position :
Location:
Channel :
Notes:

**Y N**
Interview :
Follow-up :

---

Company :
Position :
Location:
Channel :
Notes:

**Y N**
Interview :
Follow-up :

---

Company :
Position :
Location:
Channel :
Notes:

**Y N**
Interview :
Follow-up :

# Job Application Tracker

Company :
Position :
Location:
Channel :
Notes:

**Y N**
**Interview :**
**Follow-up :**

Company :
Position :
Location:
Channel :
Notes:

**Y N**
**Interview :**
**Follow-up :**

Company :
Position :
Location:
Channel :
Notes:

**Y N**
**Interview :**
**Follow-up :**

Company :
Position :
Location:
Channel :
Notes:

**Y N**
**Interview :**
**Follow-up :**

# Job Application Tracker

Company :
Position :
Location:
Channel :
Notes:

**Y N**
**Interview :**
**Follow-up :**

Company :
Position :
Location:
Channel :
Notes:

**Y N**
**Interview :**
**Follow-up :**

Company :
Position :
Location:
Channel :
Notes:

**Y N**
**Interview :**
**Follow-up :**

Company :
Position :
Location:
Channel :
Notes:

**Y N**
**Interview :**
**Follow-up :**

## Conclusion

Thank you again for downloading this guide!
If you enjoyed this guide, please take the time
to share your thoughts and post a review. It'd
be greatly appreciated!
Thank you and good luck!

www.ingramcontent.com/pod-product-compliance
Lightning Source LLC
Chambersburg PA
CBHW030532220526
45463CB00007B/2804